THE LAST DAYS OF STEAM IN
LEICESTERSHIRE
AND RUTLAND

–JOHN M.C. HEALY–

ALAN SUTTON

First published in the United Kingdom in 1989
Alan Sutton Publishing Limited · Brunswick Road · Gloucester

First published in the United States of America in 1990
Alan Sutton Publishing Inc · Wolfeboro Falls · NH 03896–0848

British Library Cataloguing in Publication Data

Last days of steam in Leicestershire and Rutland
1. England steam locomotives, history
I. Healy, John
625.2'1'0946

ISBN 0–86299–614–7

Endpapers: Front, Standard class 5MT 4-6-0 No. 73141 and an unidentified Black Five 5MT passing through Loughborough Midland with an up 'Thames-Clyde Express'
– D.J. Montgomery
Back, Ivatt 2MT class 2-6-2T No. 41278 departing from Uppingham station for Seaton junction on 4.4.59 – D.J. Montgomery

Front Cover: A 4F class No. 44414 in the Uppingham bay of Seaton Junction – Colour Rail

Back Cover: An ex-London and North Eastern B1 class No. 61375 at the coaling plant at Leicester Midland yard – Colour Rail

Typesetting and origination by
Alan Sutton Publishing Limited.
Printed in Great Britain by
Dotesios Printers Limited.

Introduction

Leicestershire was one of the most interesting counties from the late nineteenth to the mid-twentieth century as it boasted a variety of lines which had sprung up as a result of the demands of industry and people's general desire for greater mobility. As a result many schemes were put before parliament, most of which came to fruition and by 1900 Leicestershire boasted several routes running north–south and west–east across the county and all had the proud distinction of serving the city of Leicester.

The lines that penetrated Leicestershire fell into three distinct categories: main, cross-country and industrial, which meant that a great variety of motive power and train workings could be seen. The two main routes, in the form of the Midland (which had two routes northwards via Leicester and Loughborough and via Manton and Melton Mowbray with a link to Syston) and the Great Central, mirrored each other in that they gave access to the East Midlands, Manchester and South Yorkshire and it was this duplication of routes which led to the latter's demise. The Great Central operated only one main line in Leicester which afforded no connections to other routes. The long and meandering cross-country route, Rugby to Market Harborough and Peterborough, cut through the southern part of the county several times on its course. Further west the Midland line afforded useful connections to those of the London and North Western at Rugby and Nuneaton. Nuneaton was the starting point of another cross-country route which served the Leicestershire coal fields and stone quarries. This ran to Burton upon Trent and Loughborough via Coalville where it joined the Leicester to Burton upon Trent line. In contrast with the industrial routes to the west Leicester Belgrave Road station marked the start of the 'Seaside Line' from where many a holidaymaker left for that well earned break in Skegness or Mablethorpe.

The county of Rutland has now been swallowed up by Leicestershire, although the south-western part of the county was a railway enthusiast's delight. The Midland main line and the splendid Harringworth viaduct dominated the skyline, under which lay Seaton station, the junction for Peterborough, Luffenham and Uppingham. On the eastern tip this diminutive county was penetrated briefly by the east coast main line. Here 'The Flying Scotsman', 'The White Rose', 'The Tees-Tyne' and 'Yorkshire Pullman' and other famous trains could be viewed thundering past.

Sadly all this now belongs to a past age when steam was king and nearly every corner of the two counties was covered by stations and served by passenger and freight services. Most of the old vestiges of steam days have now disappeared along with many of the lines and stations.

I would like to thank P. Slater of Chesham, Buckinghamshire for the various sketches included in the book.

John M.C. Healy

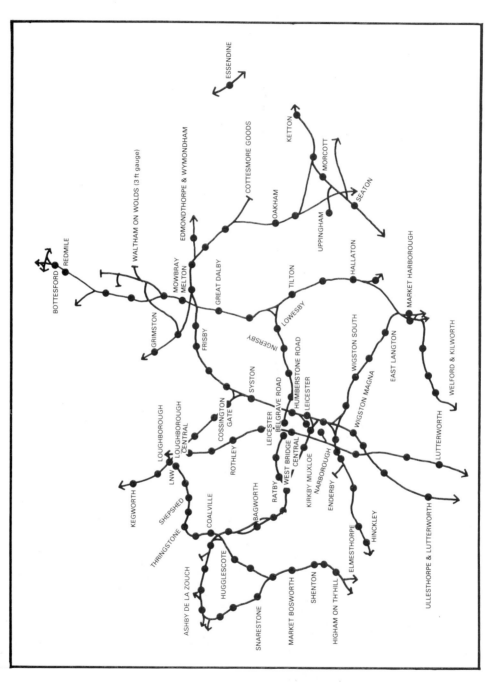

LAST DAYS OF STEAM IN LEICESTERSHIRE AND RUTLAND

Great Central Railway Route

Name of station	Opening and Closure Dates	
	Date opened	Date closed
Lutterworth	9 March 1899	5 May 1969
Ashby Magna	9 March 1899	5 May 1969
Whetstone	9 March 1899	4 March 1963
Leicester Central	9 March 1899	5 May 1969
Belgrave & Birstall	9 March 1899	4 March 1963
Rothley	9 March 1899	4 March 1963
Quorn & Woodhouse	9 March 1899	4 March 1963
Loughborough Central	9 March 1899	5 May 1969

Other details: All freight traffic was withdrawn from the line on the 12–13 June 1965 and the line ceased to operate as a trunk route from 4 September 1966. The section between Belgrave & Birstall and Loughborough Central is now used as a tourist railway.

A wooden notice depicting 'Passengers Must Not Cross The Line' from the north end of Lutterworth GCR in 1968, a year before the station closed

F.G. Cockman

An overall view of the island platform at Lutterworth in September 1959 looking north to Ashby Magna showing the cattle dock on the right, goods yard on the left and the station buildings in the middle

D. Thompson

2

One of the ubiquitous class 5MT locomotives No. 44847, leaves Lutterworth with the 5.15 p.m. Nottingham Victoria to Marylebone on 15.7.66, less than two months before long distance services on the old Great Central ceased

K.C.H. Fairey

A5 class No. 69818 works an up four coach local train from Leicester Central to Woodford Halse approaching Lutterworth on 21.5.55

J.B. McCann

Heavily laden with supporters, a fourteen coach special which departed from Leicester Central at 7.15 a.m. thunders along south of Ashby Magna on 25.5.63 on its way to Marylebone headed by 6P Jubilee class No. 45622 *Nyasaland*

M. Mitchell

On 18.5.63, a 9F 2-10-0 is seen with a train of fish empties passing Ashby Magna signalbox and goods yard after emerging from the short Dunton Bassett tunnel

Mike Marston

A close-up of the entrance, ticket office and waiting rooms at Ashby Magna seen from the road bridge above the up main line in 1965

Author's Collection

Train Service

Nottingham Arkwright Street and Rugby Central.

on and from 1 January 1968 the following service will operate.

				SO			SX
NOTTINGHAM Arkwright St. dep.	07 50	08 22	12 27	13 55	16 17	17 34	18 52
EAST LEAKE ... ... dep.	08 03	08 35	12 40	14 08	16 30	17 47	19 05
LOUGHBOROUGH Central arr.	08 10	08 42	12 47	14 15	16 37	17 54	19 12
... dep.	08 11	08 43	12 48	14 16	16 38	17 55	19 13
LEICESTER Central ... arr.	08 24	08 56	13 01	14 29	16 51	18 08	19 26
... dep.	08 26	08 58	13 03	14 31	16 53	18 10	19 28
ASHBY MAGNA ... dep.	08 41	09 13	13 18	14 46	17 08	18 25	19 43
LUTTERWORTH ... dep.	08 48	09 20	13 25	14 53	17 15	18 32	19 50
RUGBY Central ... arr.	08 57	09 29	13 34	15 02	17 24	18 41	19 59

				SO			SX	
RUGBY Central ... dep.	—	07 11	10 30	12 30	15 05	16 20	17 37	18 55
LUTTERWORTH ... dep.	—	07 20	10 39	12 39	15 14	16 29	17 46	19 04
ASHBY MAGNA ... dep.	—	07 28	10 47	12 47	15 22	16 37	17 54	19 12
LEICESTER Central ... arr.	—	07 41	11 00	13 00	15 35	16 50	18 07	19 25
... dep.	07 10	07 43	11 02	13 05	15 37	16 55	18 12	19 30
LOUGHBOROUGH Central arr.	07 21	07 54	11 13	13 16	15 48	17 06	18 23	19 41
... dep.	07 22	07 55	11 14	13 17	15 49	17 07	18 24	19 42
EAST LEAKE ... ... dep.	07 30	08 03	11 22	13 25	15 57	17 15	18 32	19 50
NOTTINGHAM Arkwright St. arr.	07 42	08 15	11 34	13 37	16 09	17 27	18 44	20 02

Notes: SO—Saturday only. SX—Saturdays excepted.

This service will provide SECOND CLASS accommodation only.

Passengers will be able to obtain tickets, between stations served by this Service only, from the Guard in charge of the train.

Accommodation will be provided for the conveyance of cycles, perambulators, etc., accompanied by passengers, who will be responsible for the removal of these articles from the stations.

Unaccompanied traffic will not be conveyed.

Season tickets, between stations served by the Service only, will be issued at Nottingham Midland, Leicester London Road and Rugby Midland Stations.

From:	Notting-ham		East Leake		Lough-boro Cen.		Leicester Central		Ashby Magna		Lutter-worth		Rugby Central	
To:	S	R	S	R	S	R	S	R	S	R	S	R	S	R
Nottingham ...	-	-	2/6	3/9	3/9	5/-	6/3	7/6	8/9	11/-	9/9	13/6	11/9	16/-
East Leake ...	2/6	3/9	-	-	1/4	2/6	4/3	5/6	6/6	10/-	7/9	12/-	9/6	14/6
Loughboro Central	3/9	5/-	1/4	2/6	-	-	2/9	4/6	5/6	9/-	6/3	11/3	8/3	14/3
Leicester Central	6/3	7/6	4/3	5/6	2/9	4/6	-	-	2/9	4/9	4/-	6/3	5/6	9/-
Ashby Magna	8/9	11/-	6/6	10/-	5/6	9/-	2/9	4/9	-	-	1/2	2/3	3/-	5/6
Lutterworth	9/9	13/6	7/9	12/-	6/3	11/3	4/-	6/3	1/2	2/3	-	-	2/-	3/9
Rugby Central	11/9	16/-	9/6	14/6	8/3	14/3	5/6	9/-	3/-	5/6	2/-	3/9	-	-

The return fare quoted above is that for Cheap Day Return.

Issued by British Railways
Divisional Manager, Furlong House,
Middle Furlong Road, Nottingham.

London Midland Region

AD136X   BR 35000   December, 1967

The timetable for the last days of services on the Great Central main line showing departures from Ashby Magna station which closed to passengers on 5.5.69

Author's Collection

6

An overall view of the deserted island platform at Ashby Magna showing the toilet block and cycle shed, waiting rooms, ticket office and entrance from the road above

Author's Collection

A3 4-6-2 No. 4472 *Flying Scotsman* roars past Ashby Magna with the GMRS 'Isle of Wight Special' on 18.5.63. Note the Pullman car, the leading vehicle, an unusual sight on the Great Central line

Mike Marston

A Leicester Central to Wembley Hill 1st Class Dining Car FA Cup Final Special coasts along near Cosby on 25.5.63

M. Mitchell

Freight on the Great Central with a Nottingham Victoria to Neasden parcels passing under the Broughton Astley road near Ashby Magna on 20.10.62

M. Mitchell

Whetstone station looking towards Leicester Central on 3.3.63, the day before its final closure to passenger services. The goods yard continued to generate traffic for a further year

D. Thompson

A train of mineral empties, with 01 class No. 63796 bound for Annesley, seen near Aylestone in 1963. These trains were nicknamed 'Runners'

John F. Clay

A B1 class 4-6-0, one of the main types of motive power on the old Great Central, is seen rushing along near Aylestone in August 1957 with the 'City of Leicester Central Holiday Express'
John F. Clay

Superpower as A3 class No. 60111 *Enterprise* heads along near Aylestone with the 'Master Cutler', one of the Great Central's main line crack express trains

John F. Clay

On Saturday 29.9.62 Standard 4-6-2 class 7P6F on an up parcels train is seen near Leicester South goods depôt on the old Great Central Nottingham Victoria to Marylebone line

H.A. Gamble

Having worked a Bournemouth to Newcastle train as far as Leicester Central, ex-GWR class 4-6-0 No. 6979 *Helperly Hall* is seen passing Leicester South goods with a Woodford Halse local service. After performing this duty the engine would run from Woodford to Banbury where it was shedded

H.A. Gamble

A sad day for the Great Central as the last through goods train comprising empty oil tank wagons from Leicester Abbey Lane sidings for Fawley heads past the Leicester South goods cabin which closed permanently two days after this picture was taken on 13.6.65

H.A. Gamble

Simmering gently by one of the water columns 4MT class No. 75062 stands outside Leicester Central shed on 22.8.62

K.C. Fairey

An impressive array of locomotives in the form of two B1 class engines and one Standard class 5 engine are seen standing on Leicester Central shed on 12.3.61

K.C. Fairey

A B1 class 4-6-0 No. 61224 pulls away from Leicester Central with a heavily laden York to Bournemouth train on 6.8.55

The late John F. Henton

A3 class 4-6-2 No. 60052 *Prince Palatine* rumbles out of Leicester Central and over the long viaduct through the city as it heads along southwards with the 'South Yorkshireman' on 6.8.55
The late John F. Henton

Unusual motive power as a B16/1 class No. 61460 waits in one of the Leicester south bay platforms at the head of a selection of old rolling stock ready to form an all stations to Woodford Halse train in 1958

John F. Clay

Simmering gently a class 5 No. 45676 waits for custom to join the 4.38 p.m. Marylebone to Nottingham Victoria semi-fast service on 10.8.64

M. Mitchell

At the head of an ICI tank wagon train BR class 9F No. 92132 thunders past a busy Leicester Central station while ex-LMS class 7P No. 46143 *South Staffordshire Regiment* waits to pick up the train on the left

H.A. Gamble

Under the canopy at Leicester Central A5 class No. 69809 waits for custom in platform 6 with the local service from Nottingham Victoria to Woodford Halse. Note the lavish goods facilities on the right

Author's Collection

On a rather overcast autumn day in 1962, one of the Thompson L1 class 2-6-4T's, No. 67780, is seen leaving Leicester Central with the 9.55 a.m. Rugby Central to Nottingham Victoria train

H.A. Gamble

After having brought in the Bournemouth to York in place of the usual Hall class, GWR 4300 class No. 6362 waits to return to its home territory at Banbury with a train of empty fish wagons

John F. Clay

A smart-looking Gresley 2-6-0 K3 class No. 61889 gleams in the afternoon sun on 30.5.62 as it passes Leicester North Passenger signalbox with the 4.30 p.m. Grimsby to Whitland fish train

H.A. Gamble

On the evening of 16.6.59 a rather tired-looking ex-GCR D11 Director class No. 62661 *Gerard Powys Dewhurst* arrives at a nearly deserted Quorn & Woodhouse station with a local Nottingham Victoria to Leicester Central service

H.A. Gamble

With a fine head of steam 9F class No. 92087 draws a train of steel empties up the gradient near Belgrave & Birstall on the outskirts of Leicester

M. Marston

On a winter afternoon in January 1950 an ex-Great Central 04 class engine makes light work of a train of coal wagons bound for Annesley

John F. Clay

Belgrave & Birstall island platform after the passage of the last ever passenger train on 4.3.63. The station was originally designed to serve the golf course on the left and the outskirts of Leicester but due to its siting in a cutting it never had a goods yard

D. Thompson

A fine view of the immaculately kept station buildings and deserted platform at Rothley with the 14.10 p.m. ex-Manchester London Road to Marylebone express on the right

Author's Collection

Near Kinchley Lane between Quorn & Woodhouse and Rothley an ex-Great Central 04 class rebuilt from an 05 No. 63912 coasts along with an up 'Windcutter' freight for Woodford Halse in the mid-fifties

John F. Clay

Normally class 9Fs were relegated to freight workings but here No. 92132 is seen with a relief working from the south coast passing Swithland sidings on 15.8.64. At one time in addition to the massive goods yard which served Mountsorrel Quarries, a station was planned for this site though the plans never came to fruition

Mike Marston

Photographed from the down side of the station, the picture shows the island platform and goods yard at Quorn & Woodhouse almost a month before closure on 1.2.63

D. Thompson

Ex-Great Central A5 class No. 69807 draws into Quorn & Woodhouse with a train of Gresley articulated coaches forming an afternoon local service from Leicester Central to Sheffield in 1952

Author's Collection

The time is 4.21 p.m. on Saturday 24.8.63 as class 5 No. 45708 is about to head the 2.38 p.m. Marylebone to Nottingham Victoria service under the A6 road bridge just south of Loughborough

T. Boustead

A panoramic view of the lavish passenger and goods facilities at Loughborough Central in March 1963

D. Thompson

BR 9F class No. 92090 draws slowly along by platform 2 of Loughborough Central station with an Annesley 'Runner' freight train from Woodford Halse on 1.8.57

Author's Collection

On the same date another BR 9F class No. 92094 is about to coast through Loughborough Central with an Annesley to Woodford Halse 'Windcutter'

Author's Collection

DAY TRIPS

TO

LONDON

12th September 1962 until 15th June 1963 inclusive

(EXCEPT SATURDAYS 6th, 13th APRIL, 4th MAY and 1st JUNE 1963)

THURSDAYS and SATURDAYS

RETURN FARE **26/-** SECOND CLASS

LEICESTER Central	...	...	...	... depart 9.18 am.
LONDON Marylebone ...	...	...	...	arrive 11.51 am.

WEDNESDAYS and SATURDAYS

RETURN FARE **28/9** SECOND CLASS

LOUGHBOROUGH Central	...	... depart 9.3 am.
LONDON Marylebone ...	...	... arrive 11.51 am.

Children under 3 years of age, free; 3 years and under 14, half-fares (fractions of 1d. charged as 1d.).

Return Arrangements

Passengers return same day from LONDON Marylebone as under:—
On Wednesdays for Loughborough at 4.38 pm or 9.55 pm
On Thursdays for Leicester at 4.38 pm or 9.55 pm.
On Saturdays for Leicester and Loughborough at 4.38 pm or 10.45 pm.

For details of Day Trips to London St. Pancras from Loughborough Midland and Leicester London Road—see Handbills L245/R (Adex) and L253/R (Adex) respectively

Tickets can be obtained in advance at Stations and Official Railway Agents

Further information will be supplied on application to Stations, Official Railway Agents, or to Mr. L. A. METCALF, District Commercial Manager, Leicester. Telephone 23841, Extn. 34.

September 1962
BR 35000

(PX2/Reg/Day)

Arthur Gaunt & Sons (Printers) Ltd.,
Heanor, Derbyshire.

B1 No. 61145 heads a Leicester Central to Sheffield Victoria local train across the bridge over the ex-Midland main line to Derby, Nottingham and Sheffield in April 1962

Author's Collection

Left: A British Railways London Midland Region handbill advertising days out in London for the winter of 1962 and early part of summer 1963

Author's Collection

Midland Main Line

Name of station	Opening and Closure Dates	
	Date opened	Date closed
Market Harborough (Midland)	14 Sept 1885	—
East Langton	7 May 1857	1 Jan 1968
Kibworth	7 May 1857	1 Jan 1968
Great Glen	7 May 1857	18 June 1951
Wigston	7 May 1857	1 Jan 1968
Leicester, London Road	1 July 1840	—
Humberstone Road	7 May 1857	4 March 1968
Syston	1 July 1840	4 March 1968
Cossington Gate	1 July 1840	29 Sept 1873
Sileby	1 July 1840	4 March 1968
Barrow-on-Soar & Quorn	1 July 1840	4 March 1968
Loughborough (Midland)	1 July 1840	—
Hathern	1 July 1840	1 Jan 1960
Kegworth	1 July 1840	4 March 1968

Other details: The route is still extensively used by a number of main line passenger and freight services and is currently undergoing modernization.

On 13.8.62 an 8F class No. 48181 briefly disturbs the calm of Market Harborough as it rushes
through on a Toton to Brent coal train

D. Montgommery

On a miserable wet day at the end of October 1959, a class 0-6-0 No. 43621, having drawn its mixed goods train into Market Harborough station, is seen here shunting it back into the large freight yard

B. Brooksbank

War Department 8F class 2-8-0 No. 90732 *Vulcan* is seen in between duties at Market Harborough shed on 3.10.50

B. Brooksbank

On the 1.7.55 6P Jubilee class No. 45589 *Gwalior* is seen rushing along near East Langton with the down 'Robin Hood' express train

D.J. Montgommery

A foreign visitor to the Midland main line, a Southern Region-based Merchant Navy 8P class 4-6-2 No. 35003 *Royal Mail* passes Kibworth North on a special on 1.3.64

M.D. Marston

All aboard for the cup as the 10.25 a.m. ex-Leicester London Road to Wembley Central First Class Dining Car FA Cup Final Special is seen approaching Kibworth North on 25.5.63

M. Mitchell

Here a 8F class 2-8-0 No. 48615 is seen passing Great Glen on an up freight in 1957

M.D. Marston

Approaching Great Glen on 1.6.57 a 2F class 0-6-0 No. 58035 can be seen with a not too taxing load which comprises just a brake van

M.D. Marston

The Railway Enthusiasts' Club 'The Bosworth' railtour ran on 10.4.65 and here it is seen passing Wigston Magna headed by 2MT class 2-6-0 No. 78028 which is minus its front number block

H.A. Gamble

Here a 6P Jubilee class No. 45626 *Seychelles* draws away from Wigston Magna with a four coach train forming the 5.05 p.m. (Sunday) Leicester to Kettering service

M. Mitchell

An immaculate 6P Jubilee class No. 45557 *New Brunswick* slows down as it takes the curve at Wigston North junction while working the 6.25 p.m. Kettering to Leicester London Road local service

M. Mitchell

Ivatt class 2MT 2-6-0 No. 46444 storms out of Knighton tunnel with the 5.20 p.m. Leicester to Wellingborough train on Friday 12.5.61

H.A. Gamble

Passing the site of the former Welford Road station on Saturday 23.6.62, a rebuilt 7P Royal Scot 4-6-0 No. 46151 *The Royal Horse Guardsman* charges out of Knighton tunnel

H.A. Gamble

A stranger to the Midland main line was this Merchant Navy class 4-6-2 No. 35012 *United States Lines* which was captured by the photographer near Aylestone junction signalbox on 14.6.64 after working a special

M. Marston

Summer excursions were popular from Leicester stations and here a Syston to Southend day excursion is seen passing the Cattle Market sidings having departed from Leicester London Road at 8.56 a.m. on Sunday 28.7.63

H.A. Gamble

The only visit of an ex-GWR engine to Leicester (Midland) occurred when Castle class 4-6-0 No. 7029 *Clun Castle* headed an 'Ian Allan Special' through the station on 27.3.65, seen here passing Welford Road cemetery

M.D. Marston

On Friday 13.4.62 a BR Standard 4-6-0 4MT class No 75059 is seen passing Knighton South junction signalbox with the 5.57 p.m. Leicester to Kettering train

H.A. Gamble

The rather grand approach to Leicester London Road station showing one of the two lovely arches under which vehicles passed on their way in and out

F.G. Cockman

An ex-LMS class 5 4-6-0 No. 44985 blows off violently as it leaves Leicester London Road with the 12.25 p.m. to Corby on 17.5.62

B. Brooksbank

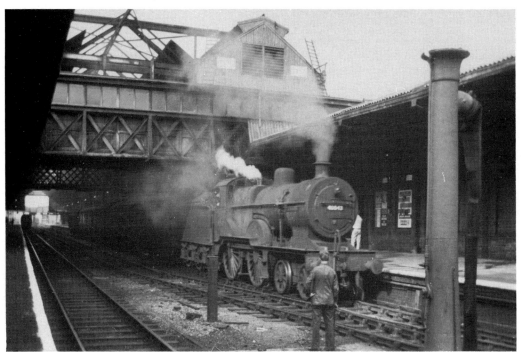

On Thursday 23.7.59 ex-LMS 2P class 4-4-0 No. 45043 arrives in Leicester London Road station with the Peterborough to Birmingham train that departed at 5.50 p.m. Note the wheel tapper
H.A. Gamble

Superpower as an ex-London and North Eastern 7P6F V2 class No. 60963 draws into Leicester London Road with a Bradford to London, St Pancras working on 12.3.61
M. Marston

Leicester London Road station and the 7.40 p.m. local service to Nottingham (Midland) preparing
to depart on 29.6.60

M. Mitchell

While a Fairburn 4MT class 2-6-4T No. 42103 waits in the sidings, a 4F class 0-6-0 prepares to leave
Leicester London Road with the 8.45 p.m. to Northampton

B. Brooksbank

On Thursday 25.7.63 an immaculate Blue Pullman set is seen working the Manchester Central to London St Pancras 'Midland Pullman' past the massive depôt at Leicester towards London Road station

J.H. Price

An ex-LMS Fowler 2P class No. 40543 is seen in the carriage sidings at Leicester London Road station on 1.4.58

Andrew Ingram

The preserved A3 class 4-6-2 No. 4472 *Flying Scotsman* draws along gently past Richards Iron Foundry, Leicester with the 'Ian Allan "Brontë" Special"' on 23.3.68

M.D. Marston

An ex-LMS 6P Jubilee class No. 45573 *Newfoundland* stands at the back of Leicester London Road motive power depôt with a couple of other engines on 2.4.65. Judging by the rather dirty condition of the engine, with shed plate hanging off, her days are numbered

D. Montgommery

A superb view of the sidings in front of the locomotive shed near Leicester London Road station with several engines in the foreground. In the background a couple of trains carrying loco coal and some old carriages used as stores vans can be seen

H.A. Gamble

Leicester London Road locomotive shed looking north. The coaling stage can be seen towards the middle with the stabling sidings and main lines to the right and goods depôt on the left

B. Brooksbank

Almost dwarfing the engines below is the enormous coaling tower at Leicester, London Road,
17.5.62. To fill the engines a wagon-load of coal was placed under the covering at the top left of the
tower, winched up the guide rails and then over, allowing the contents to drop into the tender
below

B. Brooksbank

An enthusiasts' delight in this overall view of the loco yard at Leicester, London Road, photographed on 29.9.57

B. Brooksbank

A superb view of the roundhouse at Leicester Midland depôt in 1956, ten years after opening. The shed closed in 1966 with the demise of steam

M.D. Marston

Just the job for a busy engine as 6P Jubilee class No. 45573 *Newfoundland* takes a well earned rest at Leicester London Road motive power depôt on 9.10.63

G.W. Sharpe

Leicester London Road shed's last passenger working with Stanier 8F class 2-8-0 No. 48467 in charge of the Railway Correspondent's and Travel Society's Northampton to Manchester to Crewe railtour, seen here passing Humberstone Road on Saturday 26.3.66

H.A. Gamble

51

Syston South junction and an up express coal train just passing the signalbox in 1958 headed by an ex-LMS 8F class 2-8-0 No. 48082

Andrew Ingram

A second shot of the same train, only this time the photographer has captured it as it winds round the curved Syston South junction and onto the Midland main line to Leicester London Road and London St Pancras

Andrew Ingram

The old order meets the new as an unidentified 8F class engine waits for a Birmingham Railway Carriage and Wagon three-car diesel multiple unit to pass under the signal gantry at Syston South junction with a service for Birmingham

Andrew Ingram

Not too taxing for an ex-LMS Stanier 5MT class 4-6-0 No. 45083 as it shunts a guards van at Syston North junction during 1958

Andrew Ingram

An ex-LMS Fowler 4F class No. 44602 (with a high-sided tender) is seen here ambling past Syston junction with a mixed goods train on 23.6.58

Andrew Ingram

Leaving Syston on Saturday 27.7.63 a Stanier class 5 4-6-0 No. 44965 heads away from the station with the 6.48 p.m. Leicester to Peterborough train

H.A. Gamble

Syston station with the last Midland and Great Northern up Leicester train on Saturday 28.2.59, headed by Ivatt 4MT class 2-6-0 No. 43060

Andrew Ingram

An ex-Midland Railway Fowler 4F class 0-6-0 No. 43859 leaves the Melton Mowbray line and heads north with a long train of mineral empties on a fine autumn evening in 1959

Andrew Ingram

During a deserted spell at Sileby station on 13.8.60, the platforms echo with the passage of a Sheffield to London St Pancras express

B. Brooksbank

On 4.6.62 8F class No. 48359 is seen rushing along the main line near Sileby with an up train of iron ore empties

B. Brooksbank

A large engine for a large load as 9F class No. 92159 makes light work of an up mixed freight carrying petrol tankers and mineral wagons loaded with coal near Sileby on 4.6.62

B. Brooksbank

Heading towards Sileby on 4.6.62, 8F class No. 48395 makes light work of a down express freight

B. Brooksbank

One of the 9F heavy freight class No. 92134 thunders along on a heavily loaded up mineral freight near Barrow-on-Soar & Quorn on 17.5.62

B. Brooksbank

Near Barrow-on-Soar & Quorn station a 7F class G2 No. 49450 rushes along southwards with a class J up freight working on 6.10.50

B. Brooksbank

On 6.10.50 much to the delight of some of the waiting crowd at Barrow-on-Soar & Quorn station, an 8F class No. 48269 charges along with a down iron ore train

B. Brooksbank

The tranquillity and calm that is present at Barrow-on-Soar & Quorn on the London St Pancras to Leicester to Leeds line is briefly disturbed on 4.6.62 as an 8F class 2-8-0 No. 48356 heads an up freight through the station

B. Brooksbank

Pounding towards Loughborough Midland station on 6.10.50 is 6P Jubilee class No. 45648 *Wemyss* with the 11.45 a.m. ex-London St Pancras to Bradford express

B. Brooksbank

A rather splendid picture of an ex-LMS class 2F No. 58298, still wearing its old company livery, heading south on a class K freight working. Also in view on the ex-Great Central line above 04/1 class No. 63722 heads off to Annesley with a down train conveying empty mineral wagons

B. Brooksbank

After calling at Loughborough Midland, 6P Jubilee class No. 45665 *Lord Rutherford of Nelson* draws away with the 1.25 p.m. ex-Nottingham (Midland) to London St Pancras on 6.10.50

B. Brooksbank

One of the larger engines on British Railways during the 1950s was this 2-6-6-2T Beyer-Garratt No. 47970 seen running light near Loughborough Midland on 6.10.50

B. Brooksbank

On the same day another Beyer-Garratt 2-6-6-2T No. 47999 is seen with a down train comprising empty mineral wagons bound for Toton

B. Brooksbank

With the very minimum of effort 4F class 0-6-0 No. 43910 trundles along near Loughborough Midland on 6.10.50 with a class J up mineral train

B. Brooksbank

Here 6P Jubilee class No. 45665 *Lord Rutherford of Nelson* is seen easing gently away from Loughborough (Midland) after calling at the station with a Sheffield to London St Pancras via Derby working on 6.10.50

B. Brooksbank

Superpower as Doncaster-designed Standard class 5MT 4-6-0 No. 73141 and an unidentified Black
Five 5MT storm through Loughborough Midland with an up 'Thames–Clyde Express'
D.J. Montgommery

As a few admirers look on 6P Jubilee class No. 45652 thunders along south of Loughborough Midland station with a London St Pancras to Bradford express, 1.9.57

D. Montgommery

Making light work of its train 6P Jubilee class No. 45688 *Polyphemus* rushes along southwards near Hathern with 'The Midlander' on 4.8.58

Author's Collection

Another 8F class 2-8-0 No. 48182 on 6.10.50 is seen heading southwards near Loughborough Midland with an up mineral train

B. Brooksbank

Sunday 11.9.60 and the 11.18 a.m. Bradford to London St Pancras can be seen charging through Kegworth

M. Mitchell

Another Sunday working at Kegworth with the 12.50 p.m. London St Pancras to Manchester express passing through on 28.6.59

M. Mitchell

Sunday 26.6.60 and a 6P Jubilee class No. 45605 *Cyprus* heads through Kegworth with the 1.55 p.m. Manchester to London St Pancras

M. Mitchell

A lovely wintry scene as 6P Jubilee class No. 45694 *Bellerophon* passes through Kegworth with the up 'Palatine Express' working

M. Mitchell

With a mighty effort 6P Jubilee class No. 45589 *Gwalior* charges through Kegworth with a Bradford to London St Pancras express in the early 1960s

D. Montgommery

Rugby to Leicester

Name of station	Opening and Closure Dates	
	Date opened	Date closed
Ullesthorpe & Lutterworth	1 July 1840	1 Jan 1962
Leire Halt	1 July 1840	1 Jan 1962
Broughton Astley	1 July 1840	1 Jan 1962
Countesthorpe	1 July 1840	1 Jan 1962
South Wigston	1 July 1840	1 Jan 1962

The trackbed and station of the former Rugby to Leicester railway at Ullesthorpe eleven years after closure

F.G. Cockman

Another view of Ullesthorpe station showing the modern prefabricated platform that it was given and new enamel sign just before closure of the line. Although it is pleasing to note these fixtures were still in place some eleven years after closure, nature is beginning to take hold

F.G. Cockman

A sad day for the Leicester to Rugby line as one of the last trains, in the form of the Leicester Railway Society Rugby Special, calls at a snow-covered Leire Halt on Saturday 30.12.61

H.A. Gamble

A quiet moment at Broughton Astley station on the Midland Railway Rugby to Leicester line looking towards Leicester on 24.4.61. The station closed nine months later

B. Brooksbank

On 24.4.61 Fowler 4MT class 2-6-4T No. 42352 waits at Broughton Astley station with a Rugby to Leicester local

B. Brooksbank

A fine view from the fields below of Fowler 2MT class 2-6-4T No. 42352 approaching South Wigston while working the 5.31 p.m. Rugby to Leicester train on 9.8.61

H.A. Gamble

Nothing is too much trouble as one of the massive and powerful Fowler/Beyer-Garratt engines No. 47979 makes light work of an up goods as it passes Wigston South junction on Thursday 29.9.55

H.A. Gamble

The Nuneaton Midland Route

Name of station	Opening and Closure Dates	
	Date opened	Date closed
Wigston Glen Parva	1 Jan 1864	4 March 1968
Blaby	1 Jan 1864	4 March 1968
Narborough	1 Jan 1864	—
Enderby	?	?
Croft	1 Jan 1864	4 March 1968
Elmesthorpe	1 Jan 1864	4 March 1968
Hinckley	1 Jan 1864	—

Having just assembled its mixed goods train in Blaby sidings, Wigston 6P Jubilee class No. 46543 *Rodney* heads off through Wigston Glen Parva on 17.5.63

M. Mitchell

It was hardly surprising that so many freight wagons were always parked around Wigston junction as this was the point where they were sorted into trains. These would then proceed along one of the three lines that diverged to London, Rugby and Birmingham

M. Mitchell

A light load for 6P Jubilee class No. 45704 *Leviathan* as she trundles along with a wagon-load of coal near Glen Parva junction on 28.7.61

M. Mitchell

On 20.4.63 6P Jubilee class No. 45669 *Fisher* is seen thundering by Wigston Glen Parva station with a train load of empty goods wagons being returned to the West Midlands

M. Mitchell

One of the many special workings that could be seen around Leicestershire is seen here passing Wigston Glen Parva on its way to Hunstanton, having started its journey at Nuneaton

M. Mitchell

Having just passed Wigston Glen Parva, 6P Jubilee class No. 45684 *Jutland* heads off towards Leicester with the 8.45 a.m., Saturdays only, Llandudno to Leicester London Road service on 28.7.62

M. Mitchell

Off to Wembley for the Cup Final on 6.5.61 with 6P Jubilee class No. 45649 *Hawkins* in charge of a packed train that originated from Hinckley and is destined for London St Pancras

M. Mitchell

While working the 1.10 p.m. Nuneaton to Leicester London Road local Stanier 3MT class 2-6-2T No. 40104 is seen leaving Wigston Magna with its train of three coaches on Wednesday 6.7.55

H.A. Gamble

The date is 31.3.64 and though the weather was rather bad this did not deter the enthusiasm of the passengers who packed the long train being hauled along by 6P Jubilee class No. 45585 *Hyderabad* between Wigston and Blaby while on its way to Dudley Zoo

M. Mitchell

Blaby station on the ex-Midland Railway Leicester to Nuneaton and Birmingham line looking towards Nuneaton on 1.5.65

B. Brooksbank

Croft station in March 1963 with a Cravens diesel multiple unit present and lots of passenger activity

P. Slater

North-West to Loughborough

Name of station	Opening and Closure Dates	
	Date opened	Date closed
Higham on the Hill	1 Sept 1873	13 April 1931
Shenton	1 Sept 1873	13 April 1931
Market Bosworth	1 Sept 1873	13 April 1931
Shackerstone	1 Sept 1873	13 April 1931
Snarestone	1 Sept 1873	13 April 1931
Measham	1 Sept 1873	13 April 1931
Donisthorpe	1 Sept 1873	13 April 1931
Heather & Ibstock	1 Sept 1873	13 April 1931
Hugglescote	1 Sept 1873	13 April 1931
Coalville	14 April 1883	13 April 1931
Whitwick	14 April 1883	13 April 1931
Thringstone Halt	14 April 1883	13 April 1931
Grace Dieu Halt	14 April 1883	13 April 1931
Shepshed	14 April 1883	13 April 1931
Snells Nook Halt	14 April 1883	13 April 1931
Loughborough LNW	14 April 1883	13 April 1931

Other details: On the section to Coalville most goods traffic ended in 1964 apart from at Market Bosworth where facilities remained open until 1968. The line between Market Bosworth and Shackerstone is now part of a tourist railway. Beyond Coalville to Loughborough goods traffic continued until 12.12.63.

Market Bosworth station on 10.4.65 facing Nuneaton with a railtour headed by an unidentified ex-LMS Ivatt 4MT class engine. The site is now owned and run by the Market Bosworth Railway Company who operate a line to Shackerstone

R.M. Casserley

Ex-LMS Ivatt 4MT class 2-6-0 No. 43002 is just about to pass Market Bosworth on Saturday 12.2.66 as it works the WRS Midlands railtour

H.A. Gamble

The derelict and long-abandoned country station at Shackerstone on the former London and North Western and Midland Joint line facing Nuneaton on 22.5.65 some thirty-four years after closure to passengers

R.M. Casserley

The exterior of Shackerstone station on 14.4.57 when the line was still open for goods traffic. Happily this station has been preserved as part of the Market Bosworth Light Railway project

R.M. Casserley

Hugglescote station building and yard on the former London and North Western and Midland joint line, 22.5.65. After closure to passenger services many station yards were either taken over for industrial use by local merchants or the platform buildings became private dwellings

R.M. Casserley

The derelict remains of Hugglescote station facing Shackerstone on 22.5.65, long after closure

R.M. Casserley

To commemorate the twenty-first anniversary of the Leicester Railway Society, founded in 1939, a special train was run, seen here at Shepshed on 27.5.61. Note that, although the anniversary year was supposed to be in 1960 the event was held in 1961

H.A. Gamble

The Burton Line

Name of station	Opening and Closure Dates			
	Date opened		Date closed	
Braunston	1 Aug	1849	?	1959
Kirkby Muxloe	1 Aug	1849	7 Sept	1964
Desford	18 July	1832	7 Sept	1964
Ratby	18 July	1832	24 Sept	1928
Glenfield	18 July	1832	24 Sept	1928
West Bridge	18 July	1832	24 Sept	1928
Merrylees	18 July	1832	24 Sept	1928
Thornton Lane	18 July	1832	24 Sept	1928
Bagworth	18 July	1832	7 Sept	1964
Bardon Hill	27 April	1833	12 May	1952
Coalville	25 Nov	1833	7 Sept	1964
Swannington	25 Nov	1833	18 June	1951
Ashby de la Zouch	1 Aug	1849	7 Sept	1964
Moira	1 Aug	1849	7 Sept	1964

Other details: With the opening of the line to Knighton junction from Desford via Kirkby Muxloe some of the stations on the Leicester and Swannington railway were relocated and a deviation from the original route was built between Merrylees and Bardon Hill. Although closed to passengers the Burton line is still open for freight.

The 12.20 p.m. Leicester London Road to Burton train rushes along near Kirkby Muxloe on 12.4.58
M.D. Marston

As the guard closes the level-crossing gates the Railway Enthusiasts Club 'Bosworth' railtour prepares to head away from Desford station on the Leicester to Coalville line, 14.4.57

R.M. Casserley

Here a 2F class 0-6-0 No. 58209 is seen standing at Glenfield on a railtour facing the tunnel which leads to Leicester West Bridge while its passengers have a good look round the site, 14.5.57

R.M.Casserley

Ivatt 2MT class 2-6-2T No. 41321 pauses at Glenfield station, which closed to passengers in 1928 while working a Leicester Railway Society railtour on Saturday 27.5.61

H.A. Gamble

Another view of the Leicester Railway Society goods special as it pauses at Glenfield, the last station before Leicester West Bridge

M. Marston

Having collected its train together at Leicester West Bridge yard, 2F class No. 58298 heads off past the shunter, with his pole under his arm, with the Leicester Railway Society Goods Special

M. Marston

The remains of the platform and station buildings at Leicester West Bridge station on 12.5.62, nearly thirty-four years after closure to passenger services

R.M. Casserley

Although Leicester West Bridge closed to passengers prior to the era covered by this book, the station nevertheless continued to handle freight traffic until the complete closure of the line. In this view 2MT class 2-6-0 No. 78028 is seen preparing to do a bit of shunting in the yard while the shunter waits with his pole to uncouple and couple the wagons together onto the right trains

H.A. Gamble

The fireman takes a breather as the driver backs 2F class No. 58298 onto a train of mineral wagons.
These will form part of the Leicester Railway Society Goods Special

M. Marston

Having just passed a mineral train going in the opposite direction, a class 4MT 4-6-0 heads into the recently modernized station at Bagworth & Ellistown on the Leicester to Burton on Trent line, 12.5.62

R.M. Casserley

Bagworth & Ellistown station on the Midland Railway Leicester to Burton line shortly after rebuilding on 24.4.61. The modifications to the station could be considered to have been a waste of resources as the facility closed just over three years later on 7.9.64

B. Brooksbank

The disused station at Bardon Hill on the former Midland Railway route from Leicester to Burton on Trent looking towards Leicester. When this view was taken on 24.4.61 the station had been closed for just over nine years

B. Brooksbank

An excellent view of the coaling stage and turntable at Coalville Town taken from the Leicester Railway Society railtour on Saturday 27.5.61. The two engines in the background are ex-LMS 2F class 0-6-0 No. 58305 on the right and ex-LMS 6F G1 class 0-8-0 No. 49059 on the left

H.A. Gamble

The exterior of the fine station building at Coalville, 14.9.56, proudly displaying its Midland Railway parentage in the middle of the gable in the foreground

R.M. Casserley

The Main Line Link

Name of station	Opening and Closure Dates	
	Date opened	Date closed
Welford & Kilworth	1 May 1850	6 June 1966
Theddingworth	1 May 1850	6 June 1966
Lubenham	1 May 1850	6 June 1966
Market Harborough	28 June 1885	6 June 1966
Seaton	2 June 1851	6 June 1966
Uppingham	1 Oct 1894	13 June 1960
Morcott	2 June 1851	6 June 1966
Luffenham	1 May 1848	6 June 1966
Ketton	1 May 1848	6 June 1966
Essendine	1 Nov 1856	15 June 1959

It was all a waste really as Welford & Kilworth having just been spruced up, had both its platforms repaired, a set of new lamps and a copious supply of new signs attached to buildings and other fixtures only had a year and three months before complete closure took place

R.M. Casserley

A sketch of a Rugby (Midland) to Market Harborough local train as it stands at Lubenham station on 10.7.59 headed by Stanier 4MT class No. 42541

P. Slater

The former London and North Western Railway signalbox at Market Harborough which once controlled the section of the station serving the line to Northampton Castle

F.G. Cockman

An overall view of the main station building and footbridge at Seaton station as seen from the Manton road, 4.8.65

Les Hanson

A busy scene at Seaton on the same day, with a train for Peterborough departing on the right, while a fully laden train waits to leave from the bay platform with a local for Stamford. The trackless bay on the right served the Uppingham branch and in the background one can just make out the ex-Midland main line to Nottingham

Les Hanson

Seaton station on 21.4.58 with the little Uppingham branch train waiting to depart
R.M. Casserley

On Monday 15.2.65 class 2MT 2-6-2T No. 84005 arrives at Seaton with the 1.28 p.m. Stamford to Seaton auto train

H.A. Gamble

A modern image at Seaton as BR Diesel Electric Type 2 'Bo-Bo' No. 5081 enters the station with a Peterborough to Rugby (Midland) stopping train in 1960

Andrew Ingram

On Friday 6.8.65 Derby-built 2MT class 2-6-0 No. 78028, minus front numberplate, waits to depart from Morcott with the Stamford to Seaton branch push–pull set on the 9.0 a.m. ex-Morcott
H.A. Gamble

Morcott, in the now lost county of Rutland, facing Luffenham, 23.4.59. This was typical of the once ubiquitous wayside station designed to serve small communities

R.M. Casserley

At Uppingham station Ivatt 2MT class 2-6-2T No. 41278, in immaculate condition, is seen departing with a one coach push–pull train for Seaton junction on 4.4.59

D.J. Montgommery

Ivatt 2MT class 2-6-2T No. 41279 stands at Uppingham station with a push–pull train for Seaton on a summer day in 1958

Andrew Ingram

The 9.34 a.m. Seaton to Stamford push–pull train arrives at Luffenham at a leisurely pace on Monday 15.2.65 headed by BR 2MT class No. 84005

H.A. Gamble

Gresley A4 class No. 60034 *Lord Faringdon* is seen charging along near Essendine on the famous
East Coast main line, with an unidentified down express on Saturday 17.6.61

H.A. Gamble

The Holiday Line

Name of station	Opening and Closure Dates	
	Date opened	Date closed
Leicester Belgrave Road	1 Jan 1883	7 Dec 1953
Humberstone	1 Jan 1883	7 Dec 1953
Thurnby & Scraptoft	1 Jan 1883	7 Dec 1953
Ingarsby	1 Jan 1883	7 Dec 1953
Lowesby	1 Jan 1883	7 Dec 1953
Tilton	15 Dec 1879	7 Dec 1953
East Norton	15 Dec 1879	7 Dec 1953
Hallaton	15 Dec 1879	7 Dec 1953
Medbourne	2 July 1883	1 April 1916
John O'Gaunt	15 Dec 1879	7 Dec 1953
Great Dalby	15 Dec 1879	7 Dec 1953
Melton Mowbray North	1 Sept 1879	7 Dec 1953
Scalford	1 Sept 1879	7 Dec 1953
Waltham on the Wolds	—	? 1964
Long Clawson & Hose	1 Sept 1879	7 Dec 1953
Harby & Stathern	1 Sept 1879	7 Dec 1953
Redmile	15 Dec 1879	10 Sept 1951
Bottesford South	15 Dec 1879	1 May 1882
Bottesford East	15 Dec 1879	7 Dec 1953

Other details: Although services ceased on 7.12.53, a workman's train continued to run from Leicester, Belgrave Road until 8.12.56. This ceased at the end of the month and was restarted the following April. In addition a service was maintained between Market Harborough and East Norton until 20.5.57. Summer holiday trains continued over the northern portion of the route up to 9.9.62, after which the line was officially closed.

The exterior of Leicester Belgrave Road station in 1950, a couple of years after it was taken over by British Railways

I. Gotheridge

Under the canopy at Leicester Belgrave Road. This was quite a spacious station with six platforms although it only handled a few local and long distance services. Closure to regular passenger services took place on 7.12.53 After this the station saw the passage of workmen's trains until 1957 and seaside excursions until 10.9.62

Lens of Sutton

Leaving the holiday terminus with a crowded train Thompson B1 class 4-6-0 No. 61177 and an Ivatt 4MT class 2-6-0 head off with the 9.10 a.m. Leicester Belgrave Road to Mablethorpe service on Saturday 18.8.62

H.A. Gamble

The 10.55 a.m. day excursion from Leicester Belgrave Road to Mablethorpe headed by B1 class 4-6-0 No. 61285, slows down to pick up more passengers on Thursday 9.8.51 as it approaches Humberstone station

H.A. Gamble

The rather attractive station at Thurnby on the Leicester Belgrave Road line, 1.8.50

On Tuesday 19.5.64 another Thompson B1 class 4-6-0 No. 61092, draws gingerly along tender first through Thurnby and Scraptoft station with the 5.10 p.m. Leicester Belgrave Road to Colwick goods

Ingarsby for Houghton station on the Leicester, Belgrave Road line with a train from Mablethorpe thundering along to Leicester headed by a rather grimy ex-Great Northern locomotive

Author's Collection

John O'Gaunt station on the Leicester Belgrave Road route just before its closure to regular passenger services on 7.12.53. Note the poorly ballasted track and the weed-ridden state of the platforms showing that the line was considerably neglected at this time

Author's Collection

Great Dalby station in happier days as a two coach local train headed by an unidentified 3F class 0-6-0 draws into the up platform on 1.6.50

Author's Collection

A sketch of a Mablethorpe to Leicester service as it heads gently through Lowesby station in 1960

P. Slater

The signalbox at Stathern junction on the ex-London and North Western and Great Northern joint line from Leicester Belgrave Road. The box marked the point where the lines to Nottingham and Bottesford diverged

I. Gotheridge

In between trains on the ex-Great Northern Railway's Nottingham Victoria to Grantham and Sleaford line, the photographer has managed to capture a splendid view of the staggered platforms, buildings and signalbox at Bottesford, 13.7.63

B. Brooksbank

Redmile station on the Leicester Belgrave Road to Mablethorpe line after closure, when the glass had been the removed from the station canopy

I. Gotheridge

Tilton station long after closure with the rails gone and the buildings falling into disrepair
P. Slater

A 5MT class No. 45238 draws along gingerly through East Norton on the old Leciester Belgrave Road to Market Harborough line with a Railway Correspondence and Travel Society special in 1963

Colour Rail

The sad remains of Hallaton station, once a fine outpost on the Leicester Belgrave Road line, as sketched some ten years after its closure

P. Slater

Midland Melton and Syston Route

Name of station	Opening and Closure Dates			
	Date opened	Date closed		
Manton	1 May 1848	6 June	1966
Oakham	1 May 1848	—	
Ashwell	1 May 1848	6 June	1966
Cottesmore	1 May 1848	2 April	1964
Whissendine	1 May 1848	3 Oct	1955
Saxby	1 May 1848	6 Feb	1961
Melton Mowbray	1 Sept 1846	—	
Asfordby	1 Sept 1846	2 April	1951
Frisby	1 Sept 1846	3 July	1961
Brooksby	1 Sept 1846	3 July	1961
Rearsby	1 Sept 1846	2 April	1964
Edmondthorpe & Wymondham	1 May 1894	6 April	1964

From the hill above the photographer has just managed to capture Stanier 5MT class No. 44812 before it plunges into the blackness of Seaton tunnel while working a Nottingham to London St Pancras express

Andrew Ingram

Ex-LMS Stanier 6P Jubilee class No. 45618 *New Hebrides* emerges from the northern end of Seaton tunnel with a down express for Nottingham (Midland) on 7.7.58

Andrew Ingram

A splendid view from the top of Seaton tunnel's north portal as a down mineral train bursts forth headed by a Crosti-boilered 9F class engine

Andrew Ingram

Having cleared Manton station, 3.5.58, 8F class No. 48362, based at Toton, rushes along towards
Seaton tunnel with an up goods train for the steelworks at Corby

Andrew Ingram

An up coal train headed by 4F class No. 44215 thunders through a deserted Saxby station 8.4.58.

M.D. Marston

Franco Crosti-boilered BR 9F class 2-10-0 No. 92027 based at Wellingborough (Midland) thunders out of Seaton tunnel with a down goods train in the summer of 1958

Andrew Ingram

A double-header is needed on 8.4.58 for a heavy cross-country Birmingham to Yarmouth working. Nearest to the camera 4F 0-6-0 No. 44575 and Ivatt 4MT class 2-6-0 No. 43094 wait to depart from Saxby station

M.D. Marston

A super photograph of 6P Jubilee class 4-6-0 No. 45568 *Western Australia* as it thunders round the corner and through Saxby station with a down Bradford express

M.D. Marston

A sketch of the waiting shelter at Frisby station on the Melton Mowbray to Syston link line
P. Slater

A rather splendid location from a railway enthusiast's point of view. Here the Leicester Belgrave Road to Nottingham, Skegness and Mablethorpe line can be seen in the background. This passed over the ex-Midland main line to Nottingham (Midland) in the foreground, coming off which is 6P Jubilee class No. 45685 *Barfleur* with the 1.59 p.m. ex-Sheffield (Midland) to London St Pancras, 21.7.62

M. Mitchell

The new order as a Brush Type 2 Diesel No. D5360 is just about to draw through Rearsby station on 18.5.64

M.D. Marston

Sketch showing one of the station nameboards at Edmondthorpe and Wymondham station

P. Slater

Ironstone Lines

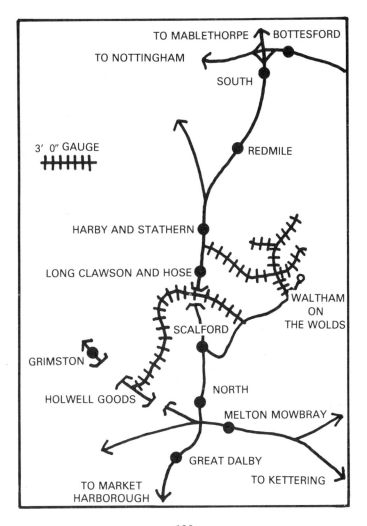

Awaiting its fate Waltham Iron Company's little Manning Wardle tank MW/10(1757) stands disused at Waltham on the Wolds, 28.8.60

R.M. Casserley

As well as the standard gauge lines in Leicestershire a number of other interesting little networks existed in the area. These were the property of the mining companies, like this 3 ft gauge line on the Eastwell Iron Company's network, 15.4.59

R.M. Casserley

Another locomotive belonging to the Waltham Iron Ore Company, *Cambrai* No. 493, stands unused at Waltham on the Wolds on 28.8.60

R.M. Casserley

Outside the shed on the Eastwell Iron Ore Company's network a 3 ft gauge Bagnall 0-6-0ST No. WB/22(2203) is being prepared for duty, 21.4.58

R.M. Casserley

A fine overall view of the Eastwell Iron Company's complex showing the loading depôt in the background and associated buildings. In the foreground on the left the little tipper wagons stand unused while on the right awaiting scrap are all the company's engines; *Belvoir, Pioneer, Mountaineer, Lord Granby* and *Underbank*

R.M. Casserley

Having worked for the last time Eastwell Iron Company's locomotive No. P/00(873) *Underbank* awaits scrapping at Eastwell depôt

R.M. Casserley

At Waltham on the Wolds on 21.4.58 a sad-looking Cranford Ironstone Company locomotive *The Baronet* about to be broken up. Note the bits of the wagons surrounding it which have already been scrapped

R.M. Casserley

Seen outside the Eastwell Iron Company's locomotive depôt, engine No. HE/36(1823) *Belvoir* stands idle on 21.4.58

R.M Casserley

The Eastwell Ironstone Company engine *Nancy* sits at the front of a train of mineral wagons as she waits for them to be loaded at the ore collection point, 15.4.59

R.M. Casserley

The transfer depôt was located at the top of the Eastwell Iron Company's incline. Here loaded wagons were sorted and sent down the incline to the standard gauge line below

R.M. Casserley